Home Staging Academy
presents ...

HOME STAGING SECRETS

The
Psychology
of
Home Staging

by

Jillian Hinds-Williams

& Tina Jesson

Home Staging Academy
presents ...

HOME STAGING SECRETS

The Psychology of Home Staging

Copyright © 2017 Jillian Hinds-Williams & Tina Jesson

This first edition published worldwide in 2017

Published by: **Lioness Publishing**
Birkdale Court, Tecumseh,
Ontario, N8N 4B3, Canada
LionessPublishing.com

ISBN-13: 978-0-9950695-3-4
ISBN-10: 0995069530

Prologue

The whole concept of preparing property for sale was and remains a tried and tested methodology in the USA and Canada. While it is still relatively new in the UK and Europe, it started to take root in London around 1999. From there it has spread out to Australia, New Zealand, and even South Africa.

Interestingly, although many picture books have been written on the subject of home staging, with impressive 'before' and 'after' shots, no one has attempted to go beyond the visual and explained the thinking behind **'why'** it works.

In *'The Psychology of Home Staging'*, you will learn the science of **WHAT** to do, as well as understand **WHY** it works too.

We explore the concept, introduce the theories, and define 20 key psychologies that when applied really do work. We have included ideas on how to market property and will identify the choices you have and the marketing problems to avoid. We have also included some very real problems people are faced with together with the answers based on 'The Psychology of Home Staging'.

This is an ideal quick reference book for anyone who deals in property, from the developer and the estate agent; to the homeowner who wants to learn more about why staging for sale shapes the way property is marketed.

According to John Batista, Vice President of National Association of Realtors (N.A.R.),

> 'I think in the near future, top producers will have to work with a home stager if they want to maximize profits and capture desired market share with little or no competition. I want to be in the forefront of this endeavor.'

CONTENTS

A little history

The whole concept of staging property for sale started in California as far back as the mid 1980s where realtors would bring in a home stylist to clean and stage the property and show people around through an Open House Event.

The stylist was usually a freelancer and earned a commission on the sale or lease of the property.

This marketing method subsequently spread throughout the major cities of the USA and Canada, with the idea arriving in the UK market in various forms in the early to mid 1990s when the British housing market went into recession and negative equity (never heard of before) became commonplace.

Why it works in North America

The North American way of life has been, for decades, based on a philosophy of 'focused' marketing and selling.

Property is no exception.

The North American culture is very much based around investment and reward. The whole idea about spending serious money on property in order to sell it for the best price aligned itself with this culture.

North Americans had been known to spend tens of thousands of dollars on a property and double their investment when they sold.

Why the American Way doesn't just work "out of the wrapper" in Europe and the UK

Transplanting the home staging concept to Europe and the UK required some slight adjustments.

The European and British cultures are still influenced by the experiences of the second world war and the post war years, which has been passed down to the following generations, and that is how they have evolved a 'clutter culture' all their own. The European culture is very much to keep **everything**, as 'you'll never know when you'll need it'.

Even now, British people think nothing of keeping a carpet for 20 years and only replacing a bed when the mattress has worn through.

As a result, it's not uncommon to find households that collect what can only be termed 'junk':

From keeping young children's clothes, to school books, to broken bikes, china given as gifts, knick knacks and even newspapers, magazines and empty jam jars!

Though of course this is not just a quintessentially British trait, as we know that older generations in all cultures experience the same 'never know when you'll need it' lifestyle.

And we're sure most people reading this will know of some relation or other who is a collector or hoarder; just as we're sure that many younger generations would be horrified to think that anyone would keep a carpet for 20 years.

So apart from clutter, why is staging for sale different in Europe and the UK?

It's all down to one thing - **budget**.

In the Europe, even people who have money want to be convinced to spend it; and spend it wisely.

The trick with the European market, if you want to call it a 'trick', is all based on making 'a **little** go a **long** way'.

Back to that inbred philosophy of the war years

Whatever the currency, whether it is $, £ or €. It all boils down to the question : Why spend 10,000 when 1,000 will do?

Why spend a fortune on a property that you are going to sell at all?

What we plan to achieve in this book is to help you to understand the psychology behind why staging for sale works, and how it can really add thousands to the value of your home.

Understanding why the psychology behind the home staging concept works will help you to target your home staging efforts, and achieve the same effects on a tight budget, without breaking the bank.

Everyone knows that 'clearing the clutter' can help - but why?

Did you know that the 'King Chair' added to a room can make it feel more welcoming. We'll tell you and why.

And even the order you show your rooms can have a dramatic effect on your buyers. We'll tell you why.

How Staging works

Buying a house is the most expensive single purchase you are likely to make in a lifetime.

You take 25 years to pay for it and the British own more residential property than most other countries in Europe.

Even so, and whether you are in Britain, Europe, USA, Canada, Australia, we still make the initial decision to buy a property within the **first 60 seconds**.

And even with second and third viewings, we make the financial and emotional commitment that this is the house we will live in and bring up our families for a number of years, by spending a total of **one actual hour in the property** (if we're lucky).

How can rational, intelligent people; doctors, teachers, dentists; normal people like you and us do this?

It seems like madness!

Then we go on to spend hundreds of thousands!

Well - it's all down to **emotions**, psychology, call it what you will, but it is definitely **not rational**.

You know when you've been to see a property and it's dark; or the bathroom is dirty and the carpet smells? It puts you off - it's not what you are looking for right?

Even if you are looking for that house as a 'do me up' and don't mind doing a bit of work on it, there are some properties that just don't 'feel' right and you're not comfortable with.

There is one key concept that we would like to introduce you to at this point. It's called the **'one year rule'**.

The One-Year Rule

If you (as a house buyer) can see yourself living in the property for the first year as it is, then you will strongly consider buying it, even if you want to change the colored bathroom suite and replace the window frames at some point.

If you can live with it for the first year you just might buy it.

Why is the 'one year rule' SO important to you?

Well, especially if you are moving up in the property chain, chances are you will be taking on a larger mortgage, larger bills, increased taxes.

The first year is usually going to be the hardest year financially when you move into your new home. The year you really find out what the new house will cost to run and how much disposable income you will have (if any).

It's only in the subsequent years that homeowners typically invest in home improvement loans, have the savings for that new bathroom, and actually consider spending serious money on their home.

That's why it's so important that in the first year, you can live with the décor and fittings you have inherited.

So, think about it from the buyers' point of view when you come to sell.

Replace that 20-year-old carpet; it could make the difference between you getting the sale or the house next door getting it instead.

We spend more effort selling a car!

Historically, we spend a bigger percentage of time, effort, and money on selling a **second hand car** privately, than we do on selling a property. We remove the scratches, replace the tires, clean it inside and out, and even replace the broken aerial.

Why?

Because we know that we can get a few hundred more for it if the car looks cared for when we come to sell.

The very same psychology can be used for selling houses too!

But in a house we can change its color by giving it a 'respray', and choosing colors that sell; by repainting the front door to give 'drive by desirability' and making extra seats or more rooms by maximizing the space planning potential and function definition.

Why Staging Psychology Matters

When you come to sell your home, you want it to look at its best.

Just as you would if you were going on a job interview, or on a date.

You would shower, wear a subtle perfume or after-shave, you might have bought a new suit and new shoes.

The same goes for selling a home.

You can't change its credentials, it's still got 3 bedrooms and 2 reception rooms (just like the qualifications on your c.v.) but you can **package** how it is presented to best effect.

The fundamental psychology is to **de-emphasize the negative** and **emphasize the positive**.

Sometimes negatives can be transformed into positives; sometimes negatives can only be neutralized to become unnoticeable, or counterbalanced by an equal or greater positive.

Like a woman who paints her lips a pale color to de-emphasize a crooked smile and using stunning eye make-up to show off beautiful eyes.

The following chapters go on to identify and describe the 20 key psychologies as unraveled through experience over our years as the leading home staging service in Europe.

20 KEY PSYCHOLOGIES

1

Let there be light

'You can never have too much light when it comes to selling a house.'

Advice taken quite literally by one property developer who installed 4 sets of double wall lights and a 3 tier central chandelier.

This is a KEY requirement of ANY and EVERY room.

Hallways must be light and welcoming; lounges well lit and spacious; kitchens and bathrooms benefit from good lighting as they look cleaner and brighter.

Too often we saw sellers presenting their properties in the gloom.

Light sells! It's as simple as that.

In Britain, with far too many grey days, even good sized rooms with lightly colored décor can look gloomy and uninviting if the lighting is overlooked. And even North American cities have grey days.

Think about new-build show homes (or model homes) for a moment; what do they do? Do they show their rooms with the lights on, or off?

Remember to use different types of lighting to define different moods for varying functions. Ambient light for relaxing in the bedroom; task lighting for the kitchen.

Ensure the light on the stairs for example is bright; use 100-watt bulbs if possible.

There is nothing more negative than ascending a dull and dreary staircase for feeling reluctant to go on.

Can you imagine doing that every night? How depressing.

FACT:

People don't buy dark houses.

WHY?

Because light represents clarity, brightness, openness and airy space.

These are all positive sensations and feelings and are very easy to achieve. It's very easy (and cost effective) to replace the darkness by adding more light.

Ensure that all the bulbs work, and replace any missing or broken ones. This is a very common problem with multi-bulb fitments and under-counter lighting in the kitchen.

Ensure the maximum wattage for your fitting. For low wattage wall lights or ceiling lights, choose multi-bulb options

Clean or replace dirty, tired looking or dated shades or fittings with bright, neutral, and modern alternatives.

Even 1980s spotlights look dated compared to the more modern streamlined chrome, which is fashionable over 35 years later.

That's another thing to remember about dating décor; **it creeps up on you.**

Some people seem to be continuous decorators; no sooner is one room finished, but they're on to the next. Some DIY addicts even change their sitting room décor 2-3 times a year. While this can be seen by many, as extreme measures, it's worth noting that interior color schemes change like high street fashion and generally only last a few years.

We still remember the vibrant reds and orange dining rooms and shocking pink bathrooms of the late nineties, thanks to bold color schemes introduced by the celebrity designers like Lawrence Llywellen-Bowen and Ann McKevit, but these soon date.

A color scheme generally lasts only 2-3 years before it starts to date.

Key rooms like kitchen and bathrooms only last around 10 years.

So it is important that if you're not the biggest DIYer in the land, and your aren't updating your color scheme every season, then you may need to do quite a bit of work before you sell if you want to achieve the maximum price on your investment. Just as you would if you didn't service and clean your car regularly.

2

De-clutter & be free ...

Pre-millennials have an inbred clutter culture.

We received more feedback from people about clutter than any other topic; "Can we come and sort out their own / their mother's / their neighbor's / their friend's clutter"

The British obsession with clutter originated from the war years, when rationing was imposed and reuse of items was a necessity.

Tina remembers her Grandmother collecting glass jars, cleaning them, and 'saving' them for jam and chutney making. A habit she never got out of, even when she stopped making the jams and chutneys. After she passed away, when Tina and her mother cleared out her cupboards, they threw out over a thousands jars! Every type of jar you could imagine, from the distinctive honey, coffee and Branston pickle jars to the Saxton's vinegar jars for pickling onions - they nearly filled an entire bottle bank.

Maybe, it was Grandma's collecting habit that made Tina so passionate about staging.

But hers was not the only family. We met many cluttered clients when home staging.

There was the lady who never threw out a single newspaper or magazine since the day she moved into her house as a newly wed back in the late 1920s. She saved the newspapers for making the fire (saving the important copies like the death of the King and the Coronation). The magazines, she saved for the knitting patterns - Women's Weekly had a lot to answer for in those days.

Then there was the lady who collected a variety of cosmetics, make-up and perfume. Half used bottles that never got thrown away and extra bottles 'just in case', filled her en-suite cupboards. Toiletries from hotels she had visited and never used. All kept as a 'memento'. All collecting dust in a basket in a corner of her bedroom. Unused gifts of expensive boxed perfume, which 'seemed a shame to use'.

These ladies are not mad, nor eccentric, but quite typical of many mothers or grandmothers who lived through the war years.

Almost in admission, we are suddenly very aware of this foible, like an alcoholic who stands up and says the dreaded words at his first AA meeting.

Car boot sales have never been more popular. And the North American Garage and Yard sales serve the same purpose.

Although those still in denial are the regular buyers.

Our new awareness of clutter, and our new mobility, now brings with it a hunger for the minimalist. Almost as if the next generations are rebelling for seemingly decades of inbred disgust at hoarding.

You don't have to be eccentric or have the same degree of clutter as the extremes we have described but things like too many photos of family and children can actually put people off. Fridges covered in magnets or family snaps, reduce the amount of white space and is just too much information to take in.

FACT:

People don't buy houses filled with clutter - no they move into EMPTY ones.

People DON'T MAKE OFFERS on houses filled with clutter.

WHY?

Because clutter is extremely personal to the owner of it. It says so much about them as an individual.

Information you don't need, and definitely don't want, when you're buying a house.

Viewers feel embarrassed, awkward and any of the 'good' positive stuff you can do is reversed by this **BIG** negative called **CLUTTER**!

Clutter is basically a distraction.

The collector of blue and white china positioned all around the picture rail in an eerie ground floor room, distracted people so much that their home stayed on the market for over a year.

The couple that viewed a house with the Agent, only to find the house belonged to an old work colleague by recognizing the people in the photographs around the house. This was extremely embarrassing and needless to say, the couple crossed the house off their list.

But beware! The extreme opposite of clutter is just as off-putting to potential buyers and that is a house that is bare and empty!

To find the right balance between being too cluttered and being welcoming and lived in, is a tricky balancing act.

Here are just a few principles to remember when decluttering:

- Take down all personal photographs
- Clean the fridge door

- Tidy and remove all but the essential items from your notice board, or remove it from the wall completely

- Thin out bookshelves, packing away all but a selection of hardbacks. Ensure all books "fit" the shelves and are ordered in size and color for an aesthetic look

- Empty bins, letter racks, and magazine racks – throw away or file

- Start to pack away all but a handful of ornaments (10 maximum). It will save you time later

- Make sure any packed boxes go either in the garage, shed or attic, and not the spare room. You don't want to turn that into the "box" room

- Sort out your clutter into the following 3 categories:
  - **Garbage** (papers, magazines, usually out of date) - dispose
  - **Broken** – fix it or throw it
  - **Unusual** – if it has not been used in a year, throw it out/make a special keepsake box of limited size so you manage this.

- Disposal methods:

  - Bin it
  - Tip It
  - Charity Shop

  - Skip it
  - Bank It
  - Car Boot / Garage Sale

- Give yourself, say two weeks, to clear it all. If its not found a new home by then, take it to the tip or recycle it through a clothes or bottle bank.

- Remove the clutter, remove the distraction that clutter causes and open your home to achieve its full value potential.

Building in a few rules to help keep you on top of clutter can also help you break the habits of the clutter culture, but that's another book!

3

Featuring the "King Chair"

Only professionally qualified Home Stagers and Feng Shui practitioners will have come across this concept – until now.

Throughout home staging we apply a select few Feng Shui concepts, and the **King Chair** is one such concept.

Some rooms can **feel empty** and uninviting, even when they have furniture or belongings in them. The reason for this is lack of a **King Chair**.

Let's illustrate…

The playroom with the collection of toys in the corner, the table pushed against the wall and shelving full of board games.

The room looks large but uninviting. A room with no welcoming seating is an "empty" room.

It has no soul, no obvious reason to use the space.

Adding a "King Chair" changes all that.

FACT:

Rooms with no *King Chair* are only *corridors* to another space.

Corridors do not have the same value as *rooms*!

WHY?

There is nothing in the room to make you want to stop and linger for a while – usually this means sitting down on a welcoming, accessible chair.

These *corridor* spaces are perceived as *dead space*, and your viewers will not be able to visualize what they would do with that space.

However, put in a *King Chair* and immediately you conjure up an image: you may imagine sitting down, reading the Sunday paper or magazine, while watching the children play, or as an escape from the rest of the household.

Make a King Chair work for you:

Standing at the door, you need to position the chair in the diagonal corner, at an angle, with the seat facing the door.

Place a cushion on it, also at an angle.

This works because the chair beckons the visitor into the room.

In Feng Shui the *King Chair* is a place of honor, reserved primarily for the head of the family – but who is more worthy of the honor than the prospective buyer that you want to impress.

The *King Chair* doesn't have to be a chair; it can be a sofa or a chaise lounge.

Note: squaring the furniture off around the walls should always be avoided, as this tends to resemble a waiting room, proper placement of furniture will encourage a more welcoming feel.

A common mistake when furnishing a conservatory is when the furniture is pushed around the edges of the space, rather than positioning seating diagonally opposite the doorway to entice people in to sit down.

Another common problem is when a dining room doubles up as a playroom and there is lack of space.

More on form and function later.

4

Free Movement

Another concept taken from the world of Feng Shui is that of
"Free Movement"

Free Movement is about allowing a free flow of energy (or Chi) through the house. If the Chi can't get through, then chances are your viewers won't either.

Let's start in the hallway

The first impression of the home, is when you come through the front door.

Coats and shoes should be put away and not left in the hall. If you have a coat rack, thin the belongings down to one item per family member and put the rest in away in a wardrobe. You want people to actually get into the place after all!

You might be selling the place for more space, but that's no reason for your coat rack to shout about it.

Maximizing the feeling of space is a must.

Let's now move into the sitting room

Did you know that British homes are some of the smallest square footage for a property anywhere in Europe? Let alone spacious countries like North America.

We visited literally 100s of British houses and all but a handful barely have space in the sitting room for the dreaded coffee table!

Dreaded might sound a bit strong, but when your viewer bangs their shin on the corner, chances are the sale will be lost.

FACT:

A property with **too much** furniture is **harder to sell** than an empty property.

As most Estate Agents will tell you, an empty property can stand on the market 3 times longer than a furnished one – so you do the math!

WHY?

It's down to lack of free movement. If you can't get around effortlessly, then the house feels too small.

Too much furniture distracts the viewer from "seeing" the rooms potential because the amount of available space is reduced.

MOVE IT TO MOVE OUT

One of the frequent problems that we saw recurring time and time again is clothing hung up behind the door.

Doors should always open fully, against the wall if possible, even if that means re-hanging them.

You don't want the door opening into the room because :

- it blocks the view of the room
- you have to walk around the door to see the space inside.

Doors that open *into* rooms rather than against a wall also take up much more space – something to take into account if you are planning an extension, doing re-modeling work or property development.

Two of our worst free movement experiences are:

1. The Victorian Semi in London that had two doors into the dining room off the lounge, and behind one was a piano!

Just by moving the piano 3ft (1 metre) into the centre of the wall allowed rediscovered access, and an attractive new visual aspect into the room through the rediscovered door, with a stunning new view of the garden, through the French doors.

The blocking off of the door with the piano, which had occurred about 25 years before, and stayed out of habit, had hidden all of the potential, so the simple solution had a transformational effect on the owner too.

2. The second was the house whose en-suite to the master bedroom could not be accessed without climbing over the bed!

The door had been hung the wrong way, and when opened, actually touched the bed!

If the Chi can't flow around, chances are your viewers won't either.

Triangular Free Movement Rule:

♦ door to window must be clear;
♦ window to King Chair must be clear
♦ King Chair to door must be clear.

5

Color Schemes that Sell

A strange concept but true.

When we talk about neutralized color schemes, we most definitely <u>DO NOT</u> mean "paint everything white".

White is far too clinical a color for the home, not to say impractical, without balancing it effectively with soft accent colors.

White does work well in bathrooms, when it can be combined with lilac, warm blues, aubergine, burgundy or terracotta.

Many people will re-decorate, at least the main rooms, prior to going on the market. But too often we saw people refreshing the paintwork in the same old "safe" color that was on the walls before.

When you come to redecorate, use this as an opportunity to select a scheme that sells.

Remember the one-year rule:

The One-Year Rule

If you (as a house buyer) can see yourself living in the property for the first year as it is, then you will strongly consider buying it, even if you want to change the colored bathroom suite and replace the window frames at some point.

If you can live with it for the first year you just might buy it.

Select a color that can last a year and will complement most furniture types.

Neutral doesn't have to mean Magnolia either. Which can look a little peachy in the wrong light.

Look at the Neutrals color charts. Hessian, Calico, and Ivory Creams combined on opposite walls will give depth and warmth.

Always paint ceilings Brilliant White.

Woodwork and Skirting should be White or Cream.

Try to remove as much dark wood or honey pine as you can. If you want to retain the look of the wood, you should opt for a lime wax or cedar wash (diluted emulsion with 2 parts water).

Lime wash can also be used on brick or faux stone fireplaces and surrounds to de-emphasize any bold dated features, and help blend it in with the rest of the décor.

Greens and Yellows are good choices for kitchens.

Consider repainting the front door (if you still have a traditional wooden type!).

A rich dark blue with new brass door furniture can look quite outstanding, and so can red or burgundy. According to Feng Shui, these colors also bring wealth and fortune (and maybe a better price) so worth a try.

FACT:
The wrong color scheme can really put off buyers.
WHY?
The thought of having to redecorate because they HAVE to, rather than when they WANT to, becomes a strong negative.

Remember the One-Year Rule!

Many people argue that people will change it anyway. And, yes, they probably will. But it will be because they want a new scheme, NOT because the old one gets them down SO much that they can't live with it any longer.

One example of this was a client who was an Interior Designer herself, who had recently had a gorgeous rich color wash applied to the whole of her hall, stairs, and landing.

Nothing wrong with that and it really did look beautiful.

The problem was that it was a strong bright orange, which is not everyone's cup of tea (or coffee) – and your potential buyer may have an aversion to orange.

The trouble wasn't just the color, either.

The strength of the color also absorbed so much light upstairs that you felt like you were potholing down a tunnel.

So the color was very strong and the lighting was poor – and the thought of getting up the stairs to repaint the highest part of the stairs and landing, would have given even the most die-hard DIY enthusiast a pause – and the cost of getting someone in, didn't bear thinking about – no wonder the house was still on the market.

In this instance, we called in a decorator, and on our recommendation, he painted out the gorgeous orange with a cream over a weekend.

The house sold to the next viewer!

6

Underfoot – Floor Facts

Flooring is an important consideration when selling a house, because it is an important consideration when buying one

One of the reasons people tend to buy "Second Hand" homes compared to new-build (in addition to more space) is that you will not have to carpet the entire home, thus saving money initially – again the ***One Year Rule*** applies.

Remember the one-year rule:

The One-Year Rule

If you (as a house buyer) can see yourself living in the property for the first year as it is, then you will strongly consider buying it, even if you want to change the colored bathroom suite and replace the window frames at some point.

If you can live with it for the first year you just might buy it.

So, if your carpet is 20 years old, you really do need to replace it!

FACT:

Poor flooring will put people off and although you may get your sale, the offer could well be lower than you could have achieved.

WHY?

♦ Old worn carpets are dangerous and need replacing;

♦ Carpets which are old tend to collect smells and can make a home smell stale and musty giving the impression of bigger problems such as damp which will be a warning sign;

♦ Dated patterned carpets can dominate the color scheme of the room and not meet the One-Year Rule.

What can be done?

It doesn't have to cost a fortune. The sitting room carpet can be replaced with a neutral Berber type with a 12 ft sq room coming in quite affordable.

Bedrooms with wooden floorboards can have their existing carpet removed in favor of a simple rug (which you can take with you when you move).

Dark colored linoleum in kitchens should be removed in favor of tile or mock tile in light colors such as white or beige.

Carpets in bathrooms should ALWAYS be removed. In many small bathrooms, melamine tiles are very affordable – and a worthwhile investment.

If carpets are less than 5 or 6 years old, in a fairly reasonable condition, and neutral in color, then it is well worth having the carpets professionally cleaned. You would be amazed how much cleaner they will look and how much fresher they will smell.

If anyone in the household smokes, or you have dogs or cats, we recommend having carpets, 3 piece suites and curtains, cleaned to eliminate these odors.

If you are looking at installing wood or laminate flooring, make sure it is of good quality, as cheaper flooring starts to split and look unsightly after a couple of years. As installation can be expensive, we do not generally recommend this type of flooring as an option for a Home Sale scheme.

The worst example we came across is when our shoes started sticking to a really dirty carpet.

One of the trickiest examples was a 20-year-old wool carpet fitted in a large 20 ft sitting /dining room, which was in beautiful condition, but the brown and orange pattern clashed with the blue sofas. The size made it too expensive for the homeowner to replace, and a new suite was not an option, so this was the only time that we ever recommended the use of throws on the seating to help blend in an old carpet.

One client was offering the carpets for an extra £350 on the price, but as they were circa 1970 – their offer was declined by the buyer.

7

Window Magic

The right window dressing can make a room, but the wrong one can completely negate all your hard work.

Competing, old-fashioned patterns with dated colors can be a real put off – and it's not just the curtains. Sometimes all that is needed is to give the windows a thorough clean inside and out to maximize the natural light into the room.

British people are obsessed with privacy and the good old British net curtain rose to popularity in the post war years of the suburban semi. Today, these look extremely dated. If you have them, we strongly recommend that you remove all nets or at least take them down and wash them.

There are modern alternatives like sheer blinds and voiles; but unless you really do need them to stop overlooking buildings looking in or to distract from a less than ideal view, then you should really take them down and open up your hose, when you are getting it ready to sell.

If "eyes are the windows to the soul", well windows are the eyes into the house.

Many people will drive by before they view a home, and it is really helpful if they can get a glimpse of your "show home" as they "drive by" to entice them in for a viewing.

FACT:

Dirty windows and dingy curtains make a house look unkempt and uncared for.

WHY?

Because if visible things like windows aren't clean, what kind of other poor maintenance is the buyer likely to find?

What about the smells that are likely to linger, maybe even damp;

Dated colors and patterns will make a negative focal point to the room.

This can be quickly and cost-effectively updated. Use of light colored tab-top curtains can bring a room bang up to date using high street products.

Likewise, white, sheer blinds can actually make the room look bigger, while maximizing the natural light into the room.

8

Drive By Desirability

Your home needs to stand out from the rest on the street.

Don't just rely on the For Sale board.

It's the <u>house</u> people want to see.

A well cared for exterior is an indication of what the interior of the house is likely to be. So, you should

- Repaint the front door and add new door furniture,

- Tidy the front garden, re-hang and oil the gate.

- Add hanging baskets or pots of flowers to make the property both eye catching and charming.

- Mow the front lawn if you have one.

- Repaint the garage door the same color as the front door to indicate it's part of the same plot.

- Make sure any wooden windows have been recently painted, and wash down frames of uPVC.

FACT:

85% of people will drive by your home before deciding to make an appointment for a viewing. Prospective buyers often cruise a neighborhood to see what they can purchase in a particular area.

WHY?

Because they don't want to waste time looking at properties that they don't find desirable, in the wrong position, in the wrong part of town, or at the wrong end of the street.

Give your house a name

Adding a name plaque or clear house number will leave your prospective viewers in no doubt that yours is the "must see" house in the area.

Next to location, giving your house a name is a sure fire way of buying an address that sells. Go for a name, which indicates something positive about the property. "Honeysuckle Cottage", or "The Croft" are good choices, but leave "The Briers" and "Nettle Grove" to your neighbor's overgrown garden!

If your home's location is not as ideal as you would wish it to be, then working hard on your home's "Drive-by Desirability" is extremely important.

Maybe you can't see the house from the road; or maybe yours is one of many for sale in the same street – so you want yours to stand out; or maybe you're located near a water tower or churchyard.

Drive-by Desirability is a key step to getting buyers through your door – so work on it

9

The "Secret Room"

Are you maximizing your "Secret Room"?

We've seen many homes that have been on the market for months, one for 3 years, which didn't follow this basic concept.

The "secret room" is basically that bedroom you just don't use anymore, or maybe you're using it as a storeroom, a box room, a junk room.

Whatever it is now, it is most definitely NOT a bedroom any longer. Thus performing the neat trick of shrinking a family-size 3-bedroom home into a tiny 2 bedroom plus junk cupboard starter home!

FACT:

Homes fail to sell if all the bedrooms are not clearly defined.

WHY?

People have a very limited imagination and a room full of junk, **never** looks big enough to be a bedroom.

There is a clue in the term "Bed" room – it needs a BED in it!

One property we visited which had been on the market for 3 years, was a dorma bungalow with what should have been the master bedroom in the roof space.

It was a very large twin aspect room with lovely views of the sea and coastline. Unfortunately, this 3-bedroom home had spare furniture piled high in this key selling area.

By moving most of the furniture into storage, by staging the unused sofa-bed as a double bed, and using the owner's best spare linen, this junk cupboard was transformed into the master bedroom and a Key selling point was re-created.

The home went on to sell to the next viewer through the door.

Are you maximizing your "Secret Room"?

Even a box room should be staged with a made up single bed, even if that's the only piece of furniture you can get in there.

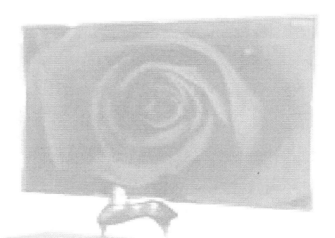

10

Accents and Highlights

Accents and highlights make a scheme friendly, welcoming, and even opulent

Earlier we talked about **Colors That Sell**, and about **Clutter** – well accents and highlights are what we use to counter an otherwise bland or bare scheme.

FACT:
When people move they are usually looking for a lifestyle to aspire to.
WHY?
They want to move up a gear and they are usually looking for somewhere bigger and better than their current home..

Accents and highlights help you to stage an aspirational lifestyle .

Bringing in a few choice accessories provides the finishing touches to a scheme and helps to bring in accent colors to a neutral room; a touch of class and opulence can be achieved by adding gold or silver frames; or add a new feature like a new window treatment or mirror. It could be a new light fitting (see Chapter 1); or a new table lamp, cushions, or a gilt framed mirror.

Another recommended way accessories can be used is as neutralizers themselves.

Cream coloured cushions, curtains and lampshades can be used to tie in a mismatching scheme without the need to redecorate. This also works for darker schemes that need light introducing to "lift" them.

Get the accessories right and you can transform a room into a very desirable selling point of the house. Choose wisely and you can recreate a beautiful scheme in your next house, when you take them with you.

11

Feature Comforts

Defining features inside each room can really make your home more
appealing.

Create a focal point in the room and make it into a feature to create an aspirational lifestyle.

If you have a fireplace, make the most of it.

All too often it's the TV that becomes the focal point of a room. Unfortunately, we have seen many a fireplace either filled by the TV or music system .

Add Aspirational Features

You don't have to invest heavily if you have a fireplace but no surround or mantelpiece.

Think creatively to create a cost effective feature. Try filling the space with pebbles or candles.

Even if you have no fireplace at all you can easily install a mantel using a thick piece of wood. A mirror can then be hung over it and a couple of large candles added to either side. Alternatively a silver shelf with 3 tall vases can add a modern feature to a room.

Windows themselves can become features in a bedroom, by introducing tied back swagged curtains to frame the window.

Adding in simple coving to a room when decorating can bring character back to older homes. A piece of etched or stained glass in a small side window or door panel can add features inexpensively.

Beds make great features in bedrooms, with contrasting throws and cushions to add that lifestyle aspiration.

Even a simple chair can be made into a feature in a corner of a room or in the hall or on a landing.

Adding a cushion or a throw or pile of contrasting towels can turn a blank corner into a feature by installing a mini King Chair.

You will see that by adding a feature, the space becomes more appealing and welcoming.

FACT:

In older homes, original house features are very desirable and can increase the value of a house by as much as 15%.

WHY?

In the UK and Europe a great deal of original features were removed from older homes post war, especially in the 50s and 60s when many fireplaces were removed or boarded over in favor of more modern day alternatives of that period.

As a consequence, because of their rarity and appeal they now add value. Even good reproductions can be used to replace the effect.

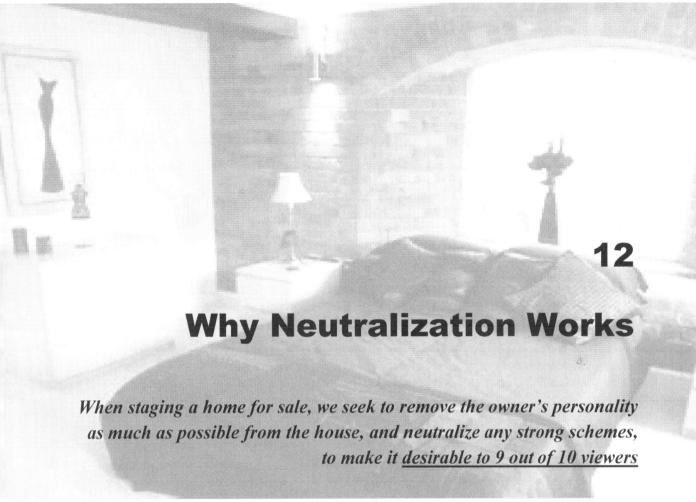

12

Why Neutralization Works

When staging a home for sale, we seek to remove the owner's personality as much as possible from the house, and neutralize any strong schemes, to make it <u>desirable to 9 out of 10 viewers</u>

Don't forget the One Year Rule

Neutralization works on the principle that the scheme will appeal to the majority.

Even if it is not to their taste, it will be inoffensive and will fit in with any furnishings they intend to bring with them.

This ties into the One Year Rule

The One-Year Rule

If you (as a house buyer) can see yourself living in the property for the first year as it is, then you will strongly consider buying it, even if you want to change the colored bathroom suite and replace the window frames at some point.

If you can live with it for the first year you just might buy it.

They may decide to redecorate but it will be because the **want** to, and not because the **need** to.

This is one of the main reasons why magnolia is used by new build developers.

Neutral accessories can be used to lighten up dark furnishings or non-matching pieces. A few new cushions replacing older, flatter accessories can breathe new life into a scheme cost effectively.

FACT:

Homes that have very bold color schemes don't sell as quickly as those with more neutral schemes.

WHY?

Because people generally don't like bold schemes; can't see how they can live with a bold scheme that might not be to their taste; would not go with their existing colored furnishings.

13

Why Personalization Fails

When creating an Interior Design Scheme we seek to personalize the décor to reflect the owner's personality and taste – a tastes that may only be shared with 1 in 10

FACT:

Homes that reflect the current homeowner's personality take three times longer to sell.

WHY?

Because people will either like it ….. or they won't.

Chances are you have limited the number of people your home will appeal to, to **only 10%** of your viewers.

The main reason why personalization doesn't work and may have a negative impact on a home sale – either by lengthening the time on the market, or reducing the value potential – is that a personalized interior scheme is just that – **personal** – and not to everyone's taste.

Take the lady with the blue and white china and faux wooden beams.

This was a good size 3 bed detached home built in the 1930s, but the chintz curtains and frilly cushions made the home very LOL (no not Laugh out Loud - but Little Old Lady).

There was a single window to the upstairs front and the real estate agent clerks referred to the house as the "Cyclops" – but more about choosing the right real estate agent later!

Needless to say, this home hung around for months on the market and as a result it didn't realize it's true value potential, eventually it sold to another LOL!

14

Scents & Sensibility

Having positive odors in a home ready for sale is very important

FACT:

Bad odors can put people off buying property.

Any sniffs of damp or moistness or pet smells can really go against your sale.

WHY?

Remember what we said about de-emphasizing the negatives?

Well bad smells are negatives, indicating trouble ahead.

We associate smell with memories, good and bad.

What we recommend is to scent the home with smells that convey warm positive thoughts – that's why the smell of baking bread and freshly brewed coffee is so popular - it may be corny but it works.

The scent of choice for selling a home is the scent of Vanilla.

This smells more like chocolate than air freshener, as most air fresheners give the impression that you are covering up or masking a bad smell – last night's curry for example.

Don't cover up though. Even vanilla may have trouble overcoming negative odors.

You still need to ensure any bad smell origins have been eliminated from the house first.

So replace damp bathroom carpeting, or buy a new pet bed, wash the net curtains, and have the suite cleaned.

Then you can start introducing some soothing positive fragrances – but keep it subtle, like a good perfume!

About half an hour before your viewers arrive, open all the windows – there's nothing like good old fashioned fresh air to freshen a room.

Then add potpourri or scented candles into key rooms, such as the lounge and bedrooms.

Never light candles or incense sticks, as the burning smell always counters the subtle fragrance of the item itself, and that's obviously a negative, as well as an untended burning candle being a fire hazard – and you don't want any accidents when your viewers are looking around.

Don't over do it. Aromas need to be subtle and not obvious, as scents should appeal to the subconscious. If someone consciously notices and comments on the smell, you've probably overdone it.

If someone does comment or they ask you what that lovely aroma is – don't admit that you can smell anything – it will make them think your house always smells that lovely.

When you clean, don't overdo it with the polish or bleach. This "just cleaned" smell can be reminiscent of the hospital, or public swimming pools. It may also indicate that before you cleaned, the house was in a right state, which is why you had to use so many cleaning products before they came. Again, open windows to disperse the newly cleaned bathroom smells.

If you do use an air freshener or vanilla spray, a great tip is to spray the fabrics in the room. Not the room. A lampshade or curtain is a good place. When the lamps are lit, the scent is released into the room, by the warmth of the bulb, providing a very subtle odor, especially good for bedrooms and hallways.

15

The Garden Room

Create an extra room outdoors

When we talk about space planning and room definition, one room that is often forgotten is the garden.

If no defined seating area is present, then large gardens can be seen as too large to manage. This is because it can be seen as a waste of space. Especially with families generally being ever more time poor, a high maintenance large space can be seen as a great disadvantage.

Just as important is the small garden, which should have a defined area to sit, eat, drink and entertain. No matter how small the space this is an absolute must, if you're going to exploit your plot's potential.

FACT:

Homes with "outside garden rooms" sell quicker and are more desirable than houses shown without a defined outdoor room.

WHY?

People today are demanding more and more from their homes. With longer hours and a more stressed lifestyle, having a space outside to "chill out" is becoming a core requirement of any home.

Eating out al fresco and the BBQ is very popular among busy professionals and families.

Even if you have a patio, lawn or decking, you still need to spend a bit of time indicating its purpose, for those occasional Spring and Summer evenings.

Even in winter, hauling the barbeque from the garage, and setting up your tables, chairs and parasol, can give a small garden or corner a defined function and actually get your viewers outside to see what they could be missing.

Adding a few tubs of bedding plants in the summer, or ivy and pansies in the winter, will add a touch of color and help define the space as a great area to entertain.

16

Brown Kitchen Syndrome

A dark reminder of the 1980s and 1990s love affair with brown and beige.

"Brown Kitchen Syndrome" is a leftover of the 1980s and early 1990s.

This is the period when brown was a popular color for many fittings.

Dark brown window frames are an indicative sign of a property from this era, and if the kitchen hasn't been refurbished since it was built; you're likely to find "Brown Kitchen Syndrome" lurking inside.

FACT:

Newly fitted kitchens in up to date colors can really sell property – and it doesn't have to cost a fortune!

WHY?

If your kitchen needs replacing, but you think "why bother? The new owners will put something in to their taste." Think Again!

A buyer will think, "that kitchen needs replacing – that's another 10k or 20k it's going to cost, plus all the time and hassle – I don't need that" and **you will lose the buyer**.

By not replacing, or at least updating, this important asset, you will appeal to fewer viewers; and take your home into the "in need of modernization" category.

Remember the One-Year Rule:

The One-Year Rule

If you (as a house buyer) can see yourself living in the property for the first year as it is, then you will strongly consider buying it, even if you want to change the colored bathroom suite and replace the window frames at some point.

If you can live with it for the first year you just might buy it.

So, if you still have "Brown Kitchen Syndrome" in your house, here are the key features you need to update:

- Brown Window Frames
- Brown Tiles, possibly with a dark brown motif on occasional tiles
- Dark oak or brown edge melamine
- Dark brown ceramic floor tiles or cork effect lino
- Brown sink

- Brown appliances (fitted eye level oven, brown microwave, brown hob, etc)
- Oh yes and let's not forget that brown "leather look" roll edged work top.

Get the point, why the term "Brown Kitchen Syndrome" is used?

In essence you can have too much of a brown thing (see Chapter 1 – *Let there be Light*, on how trends change every few years).

Kitchens really do need a re-fit every decade – in another 10 years the beech and chrome of today may well need updating to what is fashionable. No good trying to fight it – it will happen. No matter how "traditional" you go in an attempt to create a "timeless" kitchen – there really is no such thing.

Contrary to popular belief, it doesn't have to cost a fortune to keep a kitchen updated. Here are a few updates you can implement in a kitchen suffering from out of date, or Brown Kitchen Syndrome:

- Replace flooring with light beige or white diamond tile or tile effect lino.
- Replace the brown leather look worktops with a light beech or granite effect worktop, go for the real-deal granite if your budget can stretch.
- Paint the tiles in neutral white or cream tile paint. This is a great solution for well fitting tiles that are still in good condition – but preparation is key. Use sugar soap to clean away the inevitable grease you'll find on the old tiles. Use a tile primer to give the tiles a good key, as the base surface of the new color. Dark brown tiles will need one coat of primer and two coats of topcoat. This can be a time consuming job to do, as it can take up to 16 hours to dry, so leave a complete weekend to do it, and you'll be amazed at the results.
- Using multi-surface primer, you can even paint on brown melamine doors with a more modern lighter color. Try white, creams, yellow, pale greens or duck egg blue.
- Oak doors can be lightened with lime wax or a colored wood wash if you wish to retain the look of the grain. For this you will need to rub down the surface lightly with thin grade sandpaper to provide the key and lift the grain. Then apply the wood wash with fine wire wool. You can buy ready made wood wash in a choice of up to date colors. Or use 1 part emulsion to 2 parts water for your wood wash.
- Adding new blinds in pale colors can help to lighten the space.
- New LED spotlights in chrome can also bring a dated kitchen up to date
- Just simply replacing the door knobs with slim-line chrome handles or brushed chrome knobs can bring an otherwise dated kitchen into the 21st Century.
- Add under unit lighting strips to add more light into the darker corners.

- Replace kitchen accessories with up to date items - Replace the kettle and toaster with chrome options; treat your kitchen to a new washing up bowl and drainer; add a chrome fruit bowl – Don't forget all of these you can take with you.

- Replacement kitchen doors are another favorite for those with a slightly bigger budget. As long as your cupboard carcasses are in good condition, you can make a few hundreds look as though you have spent a few thousand.

- Even fully replacing a badly fitted kitchen can be done on a shoestring – especially if it is a smaller kitchen. Choose end of line units in the sales, and adding a breakfast bar counter can reduce the cost and number of units required, to give an updated look. This can be done affordably even for a complete kitchen – but you'll have to do the fitting yourself.

17

Form and Function

To drive real value out of your property you must ensure you have defined rooms or living zones, and they are shown to best effect in the house.

FACT:

Homes that have well defined living zones sell 30% quicker or realize 20% more than houses that are ill defined.

WHY?

Only 10% of the population has adequate visualization skills, so the more you can stage, the more you can show just how the home can be utilized to maximize the space available.

That does not mean having too much furniture in a home, but it does mean having furniture in each zone and defining each zone with one function.

We have seen many houses where the owners believe that by pushing the furniture up against the wall, the room will look bigger.

This is just not true. All this does is make the room look odd, like a corridor or waiting room, and it loses its function.

Dining rooms should have the table centered with the chairs put around, as if it was for dining. Setting the table can also help give the impression of entertaining.

Oversized tables should have their extra leafs removed to allow access around them from the door to the window.

If you have the space, you should consider adding a dresser, table and lamp or standard lamp in the corner. Make sure you have either a picture or a mirror along one wall that can be seen from the door.

If you only have room for table and chairs, then make them work for you, and remove all other items.

If you have your computer in the lounge or dining room, find a reasonable space for it. Define it. Add uncluttered shelving above it, to make it the computer zone of a room.

Consider packing the computer away if you don't need it for your job. It's got to be packed at some point, why not now?

Think about disguising it, by using a simple wooden screen with a fabric stretched over it to hide any unsightly area.

Make sure that any third reception room is well defined – it might be your playroom now, but stage it as a sitting room, leaving your living for best.

Ensure that all bedrooms have made up beds in each room. Make features of the bed with new bed linen, scatter cushions, and matching bedside lamps. Make a feature of the window too if you can.

If you have a dining kitchen or a breakfast kitchen, don't waste the space by adding a sofa – centre the table and stage it as a full breakfast space. Clear any breakfast bars of clutter and set it up with settings of breakfast crockery for 2, 3 or 4 people depending on the space available.

Ensure that bedrooms are staged to cater for 1 – 2 people. We have been in several properties where 3 children sleep, and the "spare" bedroom left unoccupied. Three beds in one rooms always looks cluttered as well as odd. Another negative to remove.

Much better to utilize all the rooms available to balance out the clutter.

18

Less is More ....

But minimize too far and you end up __EMPTY__

When we talk about the psychology of staging, you can see that there are many considerations.

It's not rocket science, but it does need some serious thinking and implementation if you are going to make it work to unlock your home's potential.

If in doubt follow the rule – **Less is More**.

With fewer belongings, you can maximize the space, just remember these essential points:

- **The extreme of minimal is BARE** – so start to box up your clutter, books, CDs, ornaments, but leave enough out to dress back the space, so it still looks lived in.

- **Choose your accessories carefully** - neutral ones will lighten a dark scheme or dark furniture; brighter accent colors will add subtle color to a neutral scheme and furnishings.

- **Buy a few new matching items** to introduce a theme, something modern or opulent.

- **Remove the coffee table** to allow *free movement* through the lounge – from door to window, to *King Chair*

- **Remove everything from above eye level** - this is a great tip for people with lots of items, but limited alternative available space; remove suitcases from the top of wardrobes (a very popular habit in the British home) – under the bed is a much better option if you have no wardrobe space big enough.

- **Clear out the garage and loft space** - first to allow more room for storing the things you want to keep and for any early packing you want to put away; don't use your spare room for storage.

- **Review the furniture** you have and remove any pieces that date your schemes, block any doorways, or are just unnecessary.

- **Try to even out the distribution of furniture**, so you don't have one very full room and one very empty one.

We visited one property that had 15 unmatched chairs in a small dining room. We moved some to the garage and others around the house – adding a chair to the corner of a bedroom or in a hallway and adding a cushion can be very effective; it adds a *King Chair* and eliminates *dead space*.

Dead space is that void you tend to get in the corners of rooms. It is important to eliminate dead space in these corners as it gives the room definition – like a full stop or period at the end of a sentence.

Good dead space eliminators are:

- **Lamps** – either table lamps or a small table lamp or a standard lamp

- *King Chair*

- **Plant or vases of flowers** - Each sitting room should have some form of *life* shown in it; be it flowers, plants, sticks, or natural elements like water, pebbles, or wood. This is one reason why rented and temporary accommodation (like hotels) can look so unlived and lifeless there is no *life* in the room.

Caution – don't use a cactus or other spiny plants if you want to sell. Based on Feng Shui principles, the thinking is that spiny plants look harmful and are not inviting – so avoid using them.

19

Be positive

Don't give out "bad vibes" to potential buyers.

Divorce, loss of job and death of a partner account for 74% of reasons why people are forced to move for negative reasons, with another 10% due to other reasons such as bad neighbors, house not being what they thought, intolerable smells from chemical and processing plants, or noise from aircraft or heavy traffic.

A further 16% were moving because the house was now too small for their growing family.

FACT:

According to a survey we conducted, 23% of homeowners are forced to sell for *negative reasons*.

Whatever your reason for selling you still need to be upbeat and positive about the house and the area. After all you are trying to sell it!

WHY?

People pick up on *bad vibes* or *negativity* when you are selling. And they will associate those *bad vibes* with the house.

One widowed lady said she **hated** her house so much that she felt she was tempted to "burn the place down" if she couldn't sell it quickly – not what a prospective buyer wants to hear.

Another lady who had gone through a bitter divorce, talked non-stop about the relationship her former husband had with a younger woman. He left, taking the yacht that he had worked on all their married life.

Then there was the recently bereaved gentleman who had made a gallery of photographs of his adored wife, and had tears in his eyes as he showed people around.

Owners **do** get emotionally tied to their homes.

Whatever the personal circumstances, for one reason or another they need to sell, and the act of trying to sell the property to strangers can be one trauma more than they need at this time.

So if the seller can't be positive about the good points of your home, or it is too stressful, ensure that the owner is not around for the viewings. In the UK we advised such sellers to always get their real estate agent to do all the viewings. It really can help, both the seller and the buyer.

Whether you are the seller or real estate agent showing the house. Remember these tips:

Always remember to be the only person in the house, when conducting a viewing to give the viewers your undivided attention.

That means:

- get the seller out!
- no kids,
- no pets
- no dad/mum/grandparents

What you talk about on the viewing is VERY important and knowing what NOT to say is equally important:

- **Don't mention the DIY** completed on the property. You may be proud of the fact that the shower was your partner's first plumbing job, but we guarantee, your viewers won't be impressed.
- **Don't introduce exciting anecdotes** - e.g. the time the bath overflowed and came through the kitchen ceiling or about the very expensive burglar alarm which was fitted after last year's break in!

The buyer's building survey will pick up any major problems with the house, so there is not much point trying to cover anything up, but at the same time, don't give people reasons not to at least put in a serious offer.

The seller must, however, declare in writing, any complaints that have been raised with a neighbor or if there are any disputes outstanding. Still we wouldn't mention it verbally at the viewings. Just be aware that as the sale progresses this information must be provided by law and a buyer can pull out at anytime up to signing of the contract.

Once you know how to show your property and know how much to say, there is no reason why showing the property should cause any problems.

20

It's Show Time!

The order in which you show a house is a key consideration in how the viewer's perceive it.

Selecting the best order to show the rooms in home enables the viewer to have a cohesive, rather than a disjointed viewing of the available space.

FACT:

Showing the home in the right order can make the sale, it can cost the sale if you don't do it right.

WHY?

You only have ONE chance to make a FIRST impression

That first viewing is critical if you are going to convert interest into an offer.

While an agent may not know a house as well as the home owner, they should have a trusted strategy for showing the home in the best

In the UK it is usually left to the home seller to show people around and convert that prospect into an offer.

Here are some basic rules for showing viewers around a property:

- Start with the downstairs in the BEST room – this would normally be the lounge.

- After showing the kitchen, take the viewer into the garden. Lead them down to the end of the garden so they can look back at the house. This will show how big the garden is and give a good rear view of the property. If there are outbuildings, sheds or a garage, take them through.

- Back indoors, escort them upstairs.

- Start by showing the smallest room first, and state "this is the box room/3rd bedroom" etc.

- **Always** leave the master bedroom (and en-suite) until **last**.

   That way you have a good **first impression** and you end with a **good lasting impression**.

Make of a note of these fundamental Do's and Don'ts:

- **Always** allow the viewer to enter the rooms first.

- **Never** stand in front of the window, as this both blocks the light and makes the room look smaller.

- **Do** invite the viewer to look through the window if you have a good aspect, that way you encourage the viewer to move through the rooms, hopefully absorbing all the positives you have put in place.

- **Don't** talk too much, and don't mention the words "DIY"!

- **Do** talk about local amenities, like shops, entertainment, schools, bus stops.

- **Never** say that the sale is in order move to something bigger – even if it is true, it can sound like the house won't last the buyer very long or is too small for them to consider.

The ABC of Marketing a Property

Perhaps the single biggest reason why homeowners have traditionally used a real estate agent to sell their home, rather than do it themselves, relates purely to marketing - getting the property details in front of a sufficiently large number of buyers.

A - Sell Your House Yourself?

With the advent of Internet marketing, property portals and Sale by Owner websites - do you need a Real Estate Agent to sell your house?

Even under a "sole agency" agreement, there is nothing to prevent a homeowner from advertising and selling the property privately...

...with no liability to pay commission if he /she ultimately finds a buyer without the help of their agent. Since the introduction of the Unfair Contract Terms Act in the UK, it is very rare now to find the term "sole selling rights" in an estate agent's consumer contract, meaning that individuals are still free to market the property themselves - even where they have appointed a sole agent.

The Internet provides the perfect medium for the DIY home seller to advertise his or her home at very low cost. Recent statistics show that more buyers than ever (over 80%) are looking for houses for sale online.

You don't have to be computer savvy to get your home online.

There are more and more services that offer the private seller a complete access package.

But just being 'on the internet' is by no means a guarantee that the house advertised will actually be 'visible' to the many-thousands of buyers now surfing the net for homes.

There are dozens, if not hundreds of sites that promote themselves as allowing a vendor to sell their home privately for little or no cost...

...but, before choosing a 'free to advertise' Internet home-sale service, homeowners need to consider carefully what they are likely to get 'for nothing'.

It can work - it is theoretically possible to connect to the right potential buyer - but the fact is that this remains a remote possibility with many of the sites available. You have to be careful your property doesn't stay 'a billboard in the desert'.

The problem is, that most 'free' sites are poorly marketed usually due to inadequate budgets, and rely entirely, either on advertising for their profit - which gets in the way of the message and can be off putting to buyers - or worse, selling-on registered users' e-mail addresses for junk purposes. Again this is likely to put off the majority of buyers searching for property from using such sites - the very target audience you need.

In the UK, the biggest most well-known 'free to advertise' property service, was easier.co.uk, which relied upon selling its customer mailing list for profit. Despite substantial backing which allowed it a multi-million pound advertising budget, it was forced to withdraw its free service, because it was unable to make a profit on that basis! Home sellers lost their appetite for the service when they got no viewings despite paying a flat fee. The service finally gave up the ghost and disappeared.

Many sites offer to list homes for the do-it-yourself seller, with photographs of the property, for sale boards and other bells and whistles supplied for various fees - so how do you choose?

Look for a site that firstly offers a nationwide service to sellers anywhere in your state, province or country. Most importantly, is able to attract buyers in all areas of the state, province or country. Then ask these simple questions:

- How are the house particulars presented?

- How easy is it to find and search the web site database?

- Is telephone assistance provided?

- How are buyer enquiries handled?

- Is the web site easy and attractive to use such that it will naturally draw in buyers (like bees to a honeypot)?

- How well connected is the site to the house market in general?

The internet house selling world is an extremely crowded one and search-engine /directories may not find and categorize a new website for months (if at all), so chances are few buyers will ever get to see your dedicated website.

Better to piggy-back on the multi-million marketing budgets of the industry's biggest players by using an established home selling service. But people still need to know the name of the site to be able to find it.

Most internet buyers are now being channeled by massive TV and press marketing campaigns to a handful of household names, high profile property-search services like, 'Rightmove' in the UK, Move in the US and Realtor in Canada.

These are 'portal' databases of properties held by real estate agents; normally the only way to get your property listed with these major players is by signing up to an agent's commission contract.

An interesting point revealed by recent market surveys is the fact that buyers actually prefer to deal with the seller direct, rather than through an agent - the survey found that buyers have greater confidence in what a seller tells them about the property than what an agent says. Honesty, it appears is alive and well - when preparing details, it is important to offer an honest and accurate, rather than an exaggerated description, as this is likely to be better appreciated by buyers and saves wasting everybody's time.

There is no rocket science involved in writing a property description, but when using the Internet, it is better to think in terms of "marketing" and highlighting the features of the property and why is it so nice to live there. Rather than bland "details" - try and sum up the whole property from the buyer's perspective 'in a nutshell' - preferably in the first two sentences. Once hooked on the ad, buyers will then read the detail.

Then there's the photography. 'Surf-by desirability' is vitally important when advertising online - whether you are selling yourself or through an agent. There's no point having your house's portrait up there if it looks like tired and sad, taken in bad lighting, with the neighborhood traffic in the foreground. The photographs you use can really help to reel people in OR make them move on without a second glance.

Remember, online, you're only one click away from the next house , so you really do need to draw people in.

The Internet is a great resource 'toolkit' for the private homeseller and is virtually unlimited. You can find anything from a mortgage and conveyancing, to a builder, all the services you could possibly need to get that sale moving swiftly and inexpensively.

B - Choosing Your Real Estate Agent

Typically it's the Real Estate Agent who will market your home and get prospective buyers to your door

- get this wrong and you'll have a long wait!

Tina remembers when she sold her previous property. She went into her local real estate agent's office and heard one of the advisors talking down a nearby area. That could have been her home being discussed. How would she get viewers to Tina's door if she talked to potential buyers like that. Needless to say Tina went elsewhere with her instruction.

You need to review a number of things before settling with a Real Estate Agent who is going to represent you and your little palace:

- Check their location. Is it in the high street or back street?

- Look in their window at their display. Does it look inviting, clear and draw you in?

- Speak to the staff and make sure you think of them as helpful and friendly. If not, prospective buyers could well be put off going into that office in the first place or ever going back if they do have some interest in your house.

- Look at the quality of the details they hand out. There is NO excuse for not having good quality photos on every set of details. Gone are the days when a black and white photocopy will do.

- Don't go on with the cheapest commission rate. In our experience 'cheap' commission rate means little 'work' in return and you could be waiting for months, not get people through the door and not even get your house advertised as often as with other agents. These are all areas worth considering.

- Don't automatically put your house on with the agent who has given you the highest valuation. Hard we know, but it can sometime be a ploy.

Here's our checklist for listing with a real estate agent

5-step checklist for anyone looking to put their home on the market with a real estate agent:

- Always get 3 independent valuations and go for the middle one- not the highest

- Get an idea of the value by looking at similar homes on the market which have SOLD

- If you are getting the viewings but not the offers chances are the price is right, but the presentation needs work. The expectation is set higher than the viewers can visualize.

- Make sure you have the right marketing strategy to maximize the exposure of your home.

- To enable you to afford your next home, consider spending a little time and money to realize its full potential and stage it as a show home.

There are 3 things you need to ensure are right to maximize the viewings for your house...

1. Price is right for your property type in your area

Some Agents give you a high valuation just to get your business (so beware)!

Top Tip: Check prices of similar properties in your area.

Obtain 3 valuations and take the middle one, **NOT the highest!**

2. Promotion

Ensure that the pictures you get really show off your house to its full potential. If you don't like the pictures, get them to do them again, until you're happy!

Top Tip: Internal shots can help make your house stand out from the rest!

3. Presentation

We all know first impressions count, so make sure you maximize your 'drive by desirability'!

Many viewers 'drive by' before committing themselves to a viewing.

SO MAKE THE MOST OF IT!

C - Surf Stoppers

Today, the Internet is often the first stop in the quest for buying a new house! You need your home to become a surf stopper - otherwise the next house is just one click away.

Make YOUR home stand out online - otherwise the next house is just one click away.

A study we conducted concluded that people will only make an appointment to view a house once they have driven through the neighborhood and seen the property for themselves, even if they use the Internet to find a property in the first place.

Our analysis concluded that people **don't actually buy homes** over the Internet - **they eliminate them!**

In photos or virtual tours, many homes appear cluttered, small and unattractive. Only by staging your home can you prepare your home to show it at its best.

It is vital that the photos used to promote YOUR home online are the VERY BEST pictures you can have of your home.

Don't settle for poor lighting, interior shots taken in the dark with the blinds and curtains closed, or pictures of rooms you've not prepared yet. You really will be wasting your time and hard-earned money with your agent.

You must stage your home before your real estate agent prepares your listings to ensure a faster, more profitable sale. Stage your home using the art of 'model home' or 'show home' target marketing, while tailoring each home to look "irresistible to all."

When a home is valued, the high price that is being placed on it creates 'buyer expectation', if the presentation then doesn't live up to this 'buyer expectation', the buyer will feel extremely let down and move on to the next more aesthetically pleasing house .

The process of staging creates just enough theatre to meet buyer expectation, the first step to a home sale.

You will need to identify and highlight the home's most desirable features, edit out memorabilia and personal items and rearrange furniture for the most dramatic impact possible with the space you have available.

You will need to evaluate and position lighting to create that special mood and ambience, add plants or accessories for increased 'lifestyle aspiration' ... and, when necessary bring in outside services for professional cleaning, redecorating or storage.

Only 10% of people can visualize the untapped potential in a house! Make sure your home's potential is 'seen' by the other 90%

This is the secret weapon of real estate agents and their savvy clients. It is the service that will more than pay for itself with less than 1% of the sale price yielding anywhere from 10% to 100% return on the staging for sale investment.

Home staging is extremely popular in the US, and this is what the media has to say about it:

> "In one of the nation's most expensive real estate markets where it is not uncommon to have multiple offers over asking price -- staging is fast becoming an essential part of selling a home. Home buyers are typically challenged in imagining the potential of a vacant home or the roominess of a cluttered one." - *Marin Independent Journal*

> "Dressed to sell: the practice of 'staging' homes catches on as sellers discover what it can add to the final sales price." *San Jose Mercury News*

> "The real estate industry's statistics are convincing: staging reduces

listings' average days on the market by half... and yields nearly four times as much in selling price over list price." - *Mountain View Voice*

Fact :

**" £10 or $10 spent on a tin of paint
is worth £1,000 or $1,000 on the wall"**

If a listing is not dressed to sell quickly ...

... for top price ...

IT PROBABLY WON'T!

Your Selling Questions

Answered

We see many common problems when people come to sell

Here are our top questions and answers for those who are selling

We need to sell, and get the best price possible

Jeanie asked:

We need to sell our bungalow and move down market before retirement. Although we have a detached bungalow in a good area with a large garden and we are confident that the property will sell, we really need to achieve as much as possible.

We have 3 bedrooms. Two with fitted mirror wardrobes one with Artex walls, light colored walls and skirting, light carpeting, dark wooden doors, one with sink.

During the 70s we attached beams to the lounge and kitchen ceilings. All the doors are wood stained medium oak with brass fittings as is the skirting board in the living areas.

The kitchen has American oak doors (honey colored) built under double oven, tiled work tops, spot lights, vinyl flooring, white walls.

Should we put new flooring down? I was thinking of a light wooden floor.

Do you think we should do something about the Artex ceiling and beams? Should we leave the beams and Artex ceiling in the lounge? any suggestions?

I have two medium oak settees with beige covers an oak corner dresser. We have metal patio doors in the lounge.

The house is decorated in mostly neutral colors but I have a plain red carpet in the lounge hall and dining room. Would you replace this?

The dining room has a pine table chairs and dresser and beech wood settee.

My husband thinks it's a waste of money upgrading and we'd still sell without doing anything but I'm not sure if we would achieve as much.

I would very much appreciate your suggestions.

OUR ADVICE

Your house sounds as if it could do with a bit of money spending on it to bring it up to date.

Dark wooden false beams are not in fashion as they were in the 1970s and the Artex will certainly put people off buying.

We recently made over a house who had some of the same 'features' as you describe and they really did struggle to sell before they called in a professional home stager.

It sounds like you know exactly what needs doing and we hope we can be of help to persuade your hubby to take note.

One of our clients had been on the market for 3 years, another was asked by the Agent to reduce the price by £35,000 and another, who took on advice got £10,000 more than expected.

Keep the replacement carpet to a cost-effective option - go for a neutral Berber in light beige.

Go for a pale lino in the kitchen and take up any carpet you have in the bathroom too and replace with lino tiles.

Good Luck!

Should I convert my extra kitchen back into a bedroom before I sell?

Martin asked:

I have a three bed terrace which I converted the small room into a kitchen some years ago to rent.

I'm now planning to sell, do I leave the kitchen in or do I return the property to its original three beds, I would appreciate your advice.

OUR ADVICE

It really depends if you have converted the property into two discrete flats or not (with two bathrooms). If you sell it as it stands, who would be your prospective buyer? Would you only be targeting someone looking to 'buy to let' or to 'share'? Is there a sitting tenant? This would limit your buyer base.

More bedrooms will return a higher valuation as larger spaces are always more sought after.

If it's not two discrete flats, having a bedroom as a kitchen would look very 'odd' if it was left 'as is'. 'Odd' is a negative you need to remove.

Our advice would be to return the room to a bedroom before you put it on the market and push it toward people wanting to move out of one bedroom flats.

We are trying to sell our empty cottage, should we stage the rooms or leave empty?

Cheryl asked:

We have moved out of the cottage we are trying to sell.

It has no furniture only bits and pieces, like dried flowers and wicker baskets etc.

What can I do to make it look more attractive and cozy?

Is it better, in your opinion, to stage the rooms as if they are still lived in, or leave all rooms empty, so they look larger ?

OUR ADVICE

Hi Cheryl,

This is a good question, which we get asked a lot.

What can you do to improve the presentation?

Well remove those dried flowers - I know it's a Feng Shui thing but it makes sense - dead flowers do not give a positive impression. They will remind the viewer that the house is empty. They also collect the dust, so at a minimum remove these.

Add a vase or two of paper/fabric flowers. There are some good choices from garden centers. Choose cream lilies with large green leaves for best effect and a touch of opulence.

It's often not practical to leave a property furnished, but try to ensure that the place is warm well before any viewers arrive (especially in winter months).

Make sure you leave a gilt-framed mirror over the mantle to keep a focal point to the room. If you have a couple of large candlesticks, use them to balance the mantle.

Leave potpourri and scented candles in staged places. This can add a welcoming smell rather than unwelcoming empty smell you can get.

Use Vanilla scent, as it is a rich odor reminiscent of chocolate rather than any strong air freshener that can smell like you are masking something unpleasant.

Empty or staged? Well a staged room will 'win' over an empty one any day - you just have to think of those lovely show homes you see.

Hope this gives you some ideas on helping you sell.

Good Luck!

Should we pay to make substantial repairs in order to sell our detached family home in the city or put it on the market at a reduced price as is?

Ms Showell asked:

My father has recently passed away and my mother would now like to sell their 1960s built detached family home.

The only problem is that as my father was very ill the property has not been well maintained over recent years and is in quite a poor condition.

We think that there are a number of major and costly jobs that need doing including the replacement of the garage roof and wall and a large terrace in the garden, which needs extensive rebuilding work.

I was wondering whether it is necessary for my mother to pay for all of these things to be repaired in order to sell the property or to put it on the market at a reduced price as is?

My parents' home is in a desirable location in the city and the houses in the area command quite high prices, but most of the neighboring houses are expensively maintained, we are not sure if this is a help or a hindrance?

OUR ADVICE

Dear Ms Showell,

Firstly, may we say how very sorry we are to hear that you and your mother have gone through such a sad loss.

In times like these the additional stress of having to sell the family home can be overwhelming. We're sure your mother is reassured by her caring daughter.

As far as selling the property is concerned, you have already indicated that you know and appreciate that in its current condition the property will not reach its full potential and that is fine.

It sounds as if the property is in a good location and there will always be a property developer that will seize the opportunity to make the necessary alterations and undertake the maintenance to achieve the market rate.

We suggest that you contact 3 local agents and look at the optimistic and realistic pricing they will give you.

Then we suggest you call in a couple of local builders to price out the work you think needs to be done.

Get written quotes.

Take the middle valuation and subtract the value of identified works. This will help you to ensure the price isn't too low. You will need to decide how quickly you do want to sell and that will have a bearing on if you decide to do any works yourself or do nothing and keep the price low.

If you do need to sell quickly, then at the very minimum call in a home staging consultant. A home stager can initially help you to declutter. Decluttering a lifetime of special treasures could be the starting point of packing for the eventual move. In addition the home stager can help you to restyle the home to present the property as it stands in it's best possible light.

Even if you decide to do the full project before selling the home stager can relieve you of the burden of project managing and coordinating all the trades until the property is ready to be finally staged.

Ultimately, your mother's circumstances will dictate the way to go.

There is no right or wrong, just the one that is right for you.

We hope the ideas we have given you help you to decide your way forward.

I want to sell my small flat in the city. It's currently in pretty awful condition - Should I do it up or sell as is?

Mark asked:

I want to sell my small flat in the city.

It's currently in pretty awful condition, and if I were buying it, I think I'd want to gut it, re-plaster, re-wire and re-plumb.

Is the cost of doing this likely to be covered by the increased price I would get, or would I be better off just selling it as is?

OUR ADVICE

Hi Mark,

If you sell a property with that amount of work needed you may end up 'giving' it way.

It's worth getting quotes for the work you think needs to be done.

Then get a valuation from 3 local real estate agents and ask them what it would be worth 'as is' and then if all the work was done.

Our feeling would be that you would get your money back (and some) as we expect the area you are in is still buoyant, but you need to get a local view on it.

Make sure you have enough funds left to redecorate, add a power shower and do up the kitchen.

These areas really DO help you sell.

How do I get more viewers?

Chris, asked:

Our house has been on the market for 10 weeks now with a local agent but we have only had 2 viewings.

Any ideas how we can generate more interest?

The agent has advertised the property 4 times in the local press.

OUR ADVICE

Chris,

In our experience, if you are not getting many viewings, it is because the price isn't meeting expectations, and/or the pictures are not doing the property justice.

There are 3 things you need to ensure are right to maximize the viewings for your house.

1. Price

Many Agents give you a high valuation just to get your business (so beware)!

This needs to be right for your property type in your area.

Check prices of similar properties in your area.

2. Promotion

It's good to see that your agent has advertised your property 4 times.

Check the online listing too, as 90% of all buyers now do their research online. Buyers don't buy houses online, but they do eliminate them. If the pictures aren't appealing or the property details aren't attractive, then the next house is only a click away.

Ensure that the pictures you get really show off your house to its full potential. If you don't like the pictures, get them to do them again, until you're happy!

Get the rooms staged before each photo session. Internal shots can help make your house really stand out.

3. Presentation

We all know first impressions count, so make sure you maximize your "drive-by desirability"!

Many viewers 'drive by' before committing themselves to a viewing. SO MAKE THE MOST OF IT!

Ensure the outside of your home is always looking it's best. Clear garbage. Repair gates, doors, fences, windows. Give the outside a lick of paint to freshen it up. Plant and maintain flowers and plants.

About the Authors

Jillian Hinds-Williams is founder of the Home Staging Academy, British Academy of Home Stagers, Home Stagers Network, and Home Stagers the UK's leading national home staging business, a business entrepreneur, property writer and editor.

Jillian has lived and worked in Germany, USA, Canada, and the UK, her background is with Blue Chip IT companies. She left the corporate world to establish a successful nationwide home staging franchise business in the UK, and developed an extensive program of training courses for home stagers, estate agents and property developers in how to present and market property successfully.

Jillian is an experienced writer, editor and trainer, and a Fellow of the Institute of Technical Communicators.

Jillian recently moved with her family from her home county of Derbyshire, in the United Kingdom, and now lives and works from her family home in Essex County, Ontario, Canada.

Tina Jesson qualified in Professional Interior Design at the National Design Academy and holds diplomas in Business Information Studies and Project Management and is a qualified training practitioner with over 15 years business experience.

Tina has provided expert advice to many of the UK's favorite property TV programmers, including: Channel 4's 'Selling Houses'; 'Location, Location, Location'; 'Property Ladder'; 'Downsize Me'; and the BBC's 'Trading Up'.

Tina is also a popular public speaker and has provided expert advice on the UK's national and regional radio stations; presenting for the BBC at national Property and Home Show events; and a public speaker at "women into business" events and network events across the UK.

Tina now lives in Central Indiana, USA, and is a regular guest expert on IndyStyle TV.

Tina and Jillian both worked for a time in North America, USA and Canada, and they successfully adapted the concept of home staging for the British market, after researching the North American approach.

Tina had first hand experience of negative equity on a property she owned in the mid 90s and first started to explore interior design neutralization techniques in 1995, before first going to market with the concept in 1999.

Subsequently Tina and Jillian set up Home Stagers Ltd, and from there the Home Stagers Network was born.

The Home Stagers Network established itself as an organization of property experts in the marketing and sale of property, in cost effective interior design upgrades and property buying, to cater for the full home ownership life cycle and specializing in maximizing the potential a property has to offer.

Tina and Jillian wrote the first training courses for the British Academy of Home Stagers, which received national accreditation via the National Open College Network. Students from Europe, North America and as far afield as Australia came to study with the British Academy of Home Stagers which was delivered in the grounds of a luxury Victorian mansion. The training program was further developed as a distance learning course, and is now available internationally online through the Home Staging Academy (homestagingacademy.com).

Jillian and Tina authored many articles on the subject of property improvement for magazines and national newspapers, and blogged on the Home Stagers web site (which won the Golden Web Awards for two consecutive years and the Community Web Award).

Home Stagers had strategic alliances with many independent real estate agents throughout the UK and Home Stagers' consultants were regularly represented at the National Association of Estate Agents conferences all across Britain.

About the Home Staging Academy

The Home Staging Academy began life as training division of the Home Stagers Network and national franchise of home staging consultants. Training was originally delivered as a residential program, in the grounds of a luxury Victorian manor house, and students traveled from around the world to study the program.

However, not everyone could afford the time or money to attend the residential training program.

So the Home Staging Academy was specifically developed to deliver the International Home Staging program of courses direct to students around the world via an online platform, and to ensure it was accessible and affordable to all.

The wholly online Home Staging Academy gives you a thorough grounding in Professional Home Staging, that is accessible to you wherever and whenever you are in the world at any time of day or night.

The modular program can be completed when students have the time to focus, whether they want to fast track in 6 days, take 6 weeks, or take more than 6 months. The student sets their own pace.

All courses are accessible from any device, from PC, Laptop, tablets and phones.

Source: http://www.homestagingacademy.com

Learn to be a Professional Home Staging Stylist with this free course, which introduces the concept of Home Staging. The course is aimed at anyone interested in the art of home staging, and anyone wishing to understand the basic principles of staging a house for sale. http://homestagingacademy.com

Color Planning for Professional Home Stagers introduces you to the key principles of color, and how it is applied when staging a home for sale. Understanding color is a basic requirement for anyone considering professional home staging as a career or business. http://homestagingacademy.com

Space & Feng Shui Principles for Professional Home Stagers introduces you to the key principles of space planning, and how you can define space to maximize its appeal when staging a home for sale. Understanding space management is a basic requirement for anyone considering professional home staging as a career or business. http://homestagingacademy.com

Lighting for Professional Home Stagers introduces you to the key principles of lighting, and how it is applied when staging a home for sale. Understanding light is a basic requirement for anyone considering professional home staging as a career or business. http://homestagingacademy.com

Decluttering for Professional Home Stagers introduces you Decluttering and Depersonalization of a home and how it is applied when staging a home for sale. A room cleared of clutter makes the room appear bigger, more relaxed and inviting, and more attractive to a buyer. http://homestagingacademy.com

Accessorizing for Professional Home Stagers in the final step in the home stagnig process and is an essential skill for a professional home stager. Well-chosen accessories balance the room, define it's function, portray a lifestyle, and enhance a home's desirability. DESIRABLE HOUSES SELL! http://homestagingacademy.com

Photography for Professional Home Stagers is a vital skill when building your home staging business. Being able to take great photographs of your work will help YOU to build a top quality portfolio, which is both a valuable record of your work, and a show piece for your talent. http://homestagingacademy.com

Handling Client Consultations for Professional Home Stagers is a vital course that looks at why client situations can be difficult and stressful, and how to handle them with tact and diplomacy. http://homestagingacademy.com

More from the Home Staging Academy coming soon:

Home Staging Secrets

F.A.Q.

Answers to Home Sellers' Most Frequently Asked Questions

The Home Staging Academy, began life as a training division of Home Stagers Ltd, a nationwide business founded by Jillian Hinds-Williams and Tina Jesson. Home Stagers delivered home staging services for over 10 years before Tina and Jillian sold the business and went on to build new successful enterprises, out of which the Home Staging Academy was born.

During their years delivering services direct to clients, they received hundreds of questions and calls for help and advice. Many of which are very much continue to strike a chord with home sellers today.

This book is a compilation of the most interesting questions, which they felt would be useful to homeowners, home sellers, home buyers Real Estate agents and home stagers.

This is a very useful pocket reference book to keep in the car, for anyone who deals in real estate, including professional home stagers and real estate agents.

If your client has asked your opinion or advice on a home related conundrum, chances are, you just might find the answers and suggestions they are looking for.

WATCH OUT FOR THIS IN 2017

For availability, visit
LionessPublishing.com and **HomeStagingAcademy.com**

More from the Home Staging Academy coming soon:

Home Staging Academy presents ...

How to Leverage your home and win

FINANCIAL FREEDOM

WATCH OUT FOR THIS IN 2017

For availability, visit
LionessPublishing.com and **HomeStagingAcademy.com**